Slipper |

For Beginners:

Quick and Easy Slipper Crochet Patterns

By

Angela Pierce

Table of Contents

Slipper Patterns For Beginners: Quick and Easy Slipper Crochet Patterns

By Angela Pierce

Introduction

The weather is getting cooler by the minute and it is vital that you take care of yourself in this bone chilling climate. Many people tend to get sick during this kind of fluctuating weather and it is caused when you don't take proper care of yourself. Wearing warm clothes is certainly the most important thing to do than anything else in this weather conditions. It is also vital is to cover your head, hands and feet. They are important parts of your body too and tend to get really cold as they are exposed most of the time. Wearing warm hats help keep your head and ears warm. Wear warm gloves to protect your fingers from freezing as exposing them in this weather can cause you to fall sick. Another important part to cover is your feet. Many people don't take proper care of their feet during winters. Covering your feet is not only necessary when you go outside but is also important when you are inside the house. A research revealed that people who wore snugly socks in bed experienced more comfortable and relaxed sleep than the ones who slept without socks on. But during winters, wearing your usual cotton socks isn't going to make much of a difference. In fact, it would take your feet a long time to get warm and may keep them cold throughout because that's what cotton fabric does. Rather, go for cosy, wool socks preferably hand-made as they keep they are better at keeping the feet warm and comfy.

Things That You Need

Crochet slippers are great options for the winters and they are incredibly easy to make. Moreover, they are extremely comfortable and can be designed in several interesting patterns for a fashionable look. They keep you warm at home and ideal to wear under your boots outside too. In this book you will find 5 easy and unique patterns for beginners to try out this winter to keep your feet snug as a bug.

Things you'll need:

1. Crochet hook (5.5 to 6 mm)

2. Yarn of your choice

3. Tapestry needle

4. Scissors

5. Embellishments (optional)

1. Chain and Single Crochet Slippers

Estimated Duration: Up to 1 hour

Patterns:

- Single crochet

- Chain crochet

This effortless crochet slipper can be made in less than an hour and will probably stay with you for years. They are ankle length for extra warmth and are designed using basic patterns. They can be made for all sizes. So here we go.

Step 1: Start off by doing 32-35 chain crochet patterns (Detailed instructions to do chain crochet is down below). This 32-35 chain crochet pattern is the base of your slipper, so the number of chains you do would vary depending on your foot size. Your chain crochet should look like a long braid once it is completed.

Step 2: Once you complete the chain pattern, start with single crochet going from one end to the other. (Detailed instruction to do single crochet is down below).

Step 3: Once you are done with the first row of single crochet, turn your work around as you reach the last two loops and begin the second row of single crochet. Remember, as you reach your third row, you should insert the needle under the entire braided stitch and not just one.

Step 4: Depending on your foot size you need to continue doing single crochet until you have the desired length and width that is fit to cover your entire foot and ankle. Once you are done with all the rows, you should end up with a rectangle or a square shaped pattern. This would be stitched later to fit around your foot. An average size slipper should be made within 36-40 rows of single crochet. So be sure to check your foot size and work accordingly.

Step 5: Place your work on a flat surface and place your feet over it to see it if it fits. Roughly wrap it around your foot to determine the stitching process. If the fit seems slightly small around the heel there's no need to worry as the yarn stretches when the slipper is worn.

Step 6: Once you are happy with the shape and size, you are going to have to secure the end of the crochet so it doesn't come undone. To fasten the end, yarn over and pull through two loops but rather than pulling the yarn half way through the loops, cut the yarn and pull it all the way and remove the crochet needle. Gently tug the yarn to secure it in place and it should be good.

Step 7: The loose end of the yarn must be about 20 inches long as it would be used to stitch the slipper as per your foot size.

Step 8: To give a decent shape and texture to your work, you need to use a tapestry need. Thread the remaining yarn into the needle. Now, fold your work in half and start stitching the heel in simple whip stitch pattern. This part is going to be you heel so make sure to secure the edges real good. Continue doing whip stitches till you reach the end.

Step 10: Once you are done stitching the heel, place your foot in the half-done slipper to check the fit.

Step 11: Now, it's time to do the toe section of the slipper, for which you are going to thread the other loose end of the yarn (remember? The one you started with?). To do the front section, start weaving the edge with the needle in an 'in and out' pattern until you reach the other end of the same side.

Step 12: Once you have weaved the edge and reached the other end, simply pull the yarn toward yourself as much as you can. This will scrunch the toe part real tight creating a snugly fit for your foot. Make sure you pull the yarn as much as you can as leaving it loose will result in a visible hole in there.

Step 13: Once you have the toe section of the slipper fixed together, stitch it close in the same whip stitch pattern to secure it.

Step 14: Once you have secured the toe section, it is time to secure the top. Hold both sides of the slipper together and continue to whip stitch until you reach the desired spot. Make sure to leave enough space on top so you can easily put your foot in and out of the slipper.

Step 15: Your slipper is pretty much done now. Turn it inside out, try it on and make adjustments if required. Do the other one in the same fashion and add embellishments like crochet flower or a bow to make your slippers look more presentable.

For beginners, here is a simple step by step tutorial on how to do chain crochet.

1. Hold the yarn string with both hands and make sure to leave out at least 8-10 inches of yarn.

2. Now, while holding the yarn, stick your index and middle finger of your left hand out and wrap the yarn around the two fingers twice.

3. Pull one loop through the other to create a big loop.

4. Insert the crochet needle inside the loop, yarn over the bigger end of the yarn and pull it through the big loop to create another loop. Gently tug it to tighten the previous loop. This is called a slip knot. Now, yarn over and pull it through the loop. Continue the same pattern until the next one.

For beginners, here is a simple step by step tutorial on how to do single crochet.

1. Start with chain crochet as per the instructions above. Most patterns are done after chain crochet as chain pattern is used to create a base for most crochet crafts.

2. So, when you reach the last chain, hold on to the loop you already have and insert the hook in the last chain loop.

3. Once you push the hook in the loop, grab the loose end of the yarn, hook it and pull it through the same chain loop.

4. Now you should have two loops on the needle. So, next step, grab the loose end of the yarn (it's also called yarning over), hook it and pull it through the two loops.

5. Again, insert the hook in the second chain loop, yarn over and pull it through the chain loop. Once you have two loops, yarn over and pull the yarn through the two loops. This is how you do a single crochet.

6. Continue until you reach the end.

2. Unisex Basic Rib Stitch Crochet

Duration: 1 hour

Pattern:

- Chain crochet

- Single stitch

- Rib stitch

Step 1: Begin by taking a soft yarn and do 30 chain crochet for adult size slippers.

Step 2: Once you are done with 30 chain stitches, go backward and do single crochet on each chain.

Step 3: When you reach the last chain, do one last single crochet and turn your work around. Now you would do a different version of single crochet. Rather than inserting the hook in the two strands braid-looking chain, you will only insert the hook in the back strand of the stitch. So here's what you would do. Insert the hook in the back side of the chain, yarn over, pull through the chain, yarn over one more time and pull through the loops.

Step 4: Continue doing the same version of single stitch until you achieve a square or rectangle shape. The best part of this single stitch version is that it turns out extremely stretchy and comfy.

Step 5: Place your work on flat surface and set your foot on it to check the size. If you think it's small, do more crochet or move on to the next step if it fits well.

Step 6: Now it's time to secure the slipper and give it shape. Since this is a basic slipper, it is easy to give this one the shape you desire.

Step 7: Using a tapestry needle, thread the loose end of the yarn and weave the smaller end of the slipper. Weave the edge in a simple in-and-out pattern and as you reach the other end, pull the yarn to close it up. This is where your toes will fit. Make sure to pull the yarn real tight so there is no visible hole.

Step 8: Once the toe is secured, hold both sides of the slipper and start whip stitching the top of your slipper. Keep stitching until you reach an appropriate spot which will allow you to insert your foot inside the slipper. So make sure you leave it wide enough so it doesn't feel too tight.

Step 9: Try on the slipper one more time and if you are happy with the look and feel, sew the heel with simple whip stitch.

Step 10: Add a flower or a tiny pom-pom on top of the slipper for a fancy look and you are done.

3. Crochet Ballet Slippers

Duration: 1-2 hours

Pattern:

- Chain crochet

- Double crochet

- Half double crochet

Step 1: Begin with a simple slip knot - Loop the yarn around the hook and hold the loose end of the yarn with your fingers. Yarn over and pull it through the loop and that's your slip knot.

Step 2: Do 30 chain crochet for adult size ballet slippers to create the base of your shoes.

Step 3: Once you are done with 30 chain stitches you are going to do single crochet in the second chain. So insert the hook in the second chain, yarn over and you get two loops on your hook, yarn over again and pull through the two loops. Go into the same chain again and do another single crochet. Once you've done that, do single crochet in each chain until you reach the other end.

Step 4: On the last chain do 3 single crochet and turn your work around.

Step 5: Do single crochet in each stitch until you reach the other end. Once again, as you reach the end, do 2 single crochet in the last stitch.

Step 6: Once you are done with 2 single crochet, do a slip knot and follow by doing 3 chain crochet.

Step 7: Now you need to do 2 double crochet in the first stitch – Here's how you would do double crochet. So yarn over, go into the next stitch, yarn over again and you should get 3 loops. Yarn over and pull through 2 loops and yarn over again and pull through 2 loops. Repeat the same pattern in the same stitch one more time and follow by doing 1 double crochet in every stitch until you reach the other end.

Step 8: On completing the last stitch, you are going to work through the corner. Do 2 double crochet in the middle stitch. Go into the next stitch and do 2 more double crochet. You'll notice that now you've reached the other side of the work.

Step 9: On this side you will do 1 double crochet in each stitch. Do this till to reach the end. After doing double crochet in the last stitch, do a double crochet in the very first chain you did. Do a slip knot and follow by doing 3 simple chain crochet.

Step 10: Now you would do half double crochet in the next stitch - Yarn over, go into the next stitch, yarn over, and pull through all three loops. Do another half double crochet in the same stitch. And now, do one half double crochet in every stitch all the way to the end. On the last stitch, do 2 half double crochet and then 1 half double crochet in each stitch all the way to the end.

Step 11: Keep your foot size in mind and until you reach the desired size, continue the same pattern.

Step 12: You should get something that looks loosely like a slipper but lacking the final stitches. When you are happy with the size, do a slip knot and cut the yarn.

Step 13: Thread the leftover yarn into a needle at the toe section of the slipper and weave the edges from one end to the other. Pull the yarn real tight.

Step 14: Join both sides of the slipper and stitch the top front part of your slipper. You can stitch half way through so you have enough room to comfortably insert your foot inside.

Step 15: Sew the Back part of the slipper and you are done.

4. Easy Magic Circle Crochet Slipper

Duration: 1 to 1.5 hours

Pattern:

- Magic circle

- Double crochet

Step 1: Start by taking two strands of yarn as this crochet slipper is going to be thick and comfy and wouldn't hurt your feet while keeping your feet warm. You can also use two different colours of yarn for added texture.

Step 2: You need to begin the slipper by doing a magic circle. If you do not know how to do a magic circle crochet, there is a step by step tutorial right after this one.

Step 3: Do double crochet 12 times around the magic circle. Do it 12 times if you have medium to large foot and for smaller foot you can do about 10-11 times.

Step 4: Once you are done with 12 double crochet, secure by doing a slip knot stitch in the 3rd chain. This slipper does not require any stitching through tapestry needle.

Step 5: Continue the same pattern like you did the when you started the magic circle. Go around the circle by following the same pattern. Continue doing the same until you complete 8-9 rows. 8-9 rows are ideal for an average size 7. As you keep going around the circle the slipper would keep expanding to fit your foot perfectly.

Step 6: Once you are done doing 9 rows, try the slipper on to see if it fits you properly. Since you'll be using two strands of yarn; the slipper would be extremely relaxing and stretchy so the fitting shouldn't be a problem.

Step 7: Now is when you will do the heel section as 9 rows of double crochet will cover your toe to the front section of your ankle. The top part of the slipper needs to be left unworked as that is where you will put your foot in and out. Determine how wide or snugly you want that opening to be and mark the spot using a stitch marker so you would know you are not supposed to touch that section.

Step 8: Now let's work on the heel and ankle section. Pick up where you left off and do 3 simple chain crochet.

Step 9: Start doing the double crochet again like earlier. Do it until you reach the stitch marker and stop there. Do 3 more chains and turn your work around from there. This will be the bottom section of your slipper. Continue doing double crochet again until you reach the other end. To complete the bottom and heel you should be doing 4-5 rows of double crochet.

Step 10: Once you are done, try the slipper on and make sure you have enough room to secure the back of the slipper.

Step 11: To secure the back of the slipper, you can either use the slip knot stitch technique using the hook needle or whip stitch method using tapestry needle. Stitch the back and you are done.

For beginners, here is a simple step by step tutorial on how to do magic circle crochet.

1. Begin with a slip knot but do not tighten the knot and leave it loose creating a circle with the yarn (one or two strands of yarn). Firmly hold the open ends of

the circle and pull two strands through the circle using a hook needle.

2. Once you grab the two strands through the loop, hook the yarn outside of the loop and pull it through the small loop you just created. It may seem a bit complicated but a little practice is all it needs.

3. Make sure to hold on to the loose end of the yarn firmly.

4. Now, yarn over another time and do 3 chain crochet.

5. The next step is to do 1 double crochet.

Here's how to do double crochet: Yarn over, go into the next stitch, yarn over again and you should get 3 loops. Yarn over and pull through 2 loops and yarn over again and pull through 2 loops.

6. So, still make sure to hold on to that big circle you created in the beginning as it is the base of the magic circle.

7. Continue doing double crochet and follow the same pattern 12 times.

8. Once you are done with 12 patterns, secure by doing a slip knot stitch in the 3rd chain.

9. Continue the same pattern as before to go around the magic circle.

5. Snugly Bootie Slipper

Duration: 1 to 2 hours

Patterns:

- Single crochet

- Chain crochet

Step 1: Start by doing 32-35 chain crochet. This is the bottom of your slipper, so the number of chains would vary depending on your foot size.

Step 2: Once you complete the 35 chain crochet, follow by doing single crochet in each stitch going from one end through the other.

Step 3: Once you are done with single crochet and as you reach the last 2 loops, turn your work around and do the second row of single crochet.

Step 4: When you reach the third row, insert the hook under the entire braided loop (the entire stitch).

Step 5: Depending on your foot size you need to continue doing single crochet until you reach the desired length and width that is good enough to cover your entire foot and ankle. Once you are done with all the rows, you should end up with a rectangle or square shaped work.

Step 6: Place your work on flat surface and place your feet over it to see it if it fits. Roughly wrap it around your foot to check if the fit is right. If not, you can make adjustments.

Step 6: Once you are happy with the shape and size, you can secure the end of the crochet so it doesn't come undone. To fasten the end, yarn the two loops and rather than pulling the yarn half way through the loops, pull it all the way and remove the crochet needle. Gently tug the yarn to secure it in place and it should be good. The loose end of the yarn must be about 20 inches long to stitch the slipper.

Step 7: To give your slipper proper shape, you need to use a tapestry needle. Thread the remaining yarn in a tapestry needle.

Step 8: Fold your work in half and start stitching the back of the heel in simple whip stitches. This part is going to be the back of your slipper so make sure to secure the edges properly. So, continue doing a whip stitch until it's completely secure.

Step 9: When you are done stitching the back of the heel, insert your foot in the half-done slipper to check the fit.

Step 10: If you are happy with the fit, get ready to do the toe section of the slipper, for which you are going to thread the other end of the yarn (remember? The one you started with?). To do the toe, section, start weaving the edge in an in-and-out pattern until you reach the other end of the same side.

Step 11: Once you are done weaving the edge, pull the yarn toward yourself as much as you can. This will scrunch the toe section real tight creating a snugly fit for your foot. Make sure you pull the yarn as much as possible as you don't want a hole in there.

Step 12: Once you are done with the toe section of the slipper is scrunched together, stitch it to secure it properly in the same whip stitch pattern.

Step 13: Once the toe section is secured, it is time to secure the top part. Hold both sides of the slipper together and continue to whip stitch until you reach the desired spot. Make sure to leave enough space on top for your foot to go in and out with ease.

Step 14: Turn the slipper inside out, try it on and make adjustments if required because once you crochet the high ankle, you won't be able to make any changes to the slipper.

Step 15: To give your crochet slipper a bootie look, you are going to crochet the ankle on your slipper. Start at the top back section of the slipper to create the bootie look. Continue doing single crochet and go around the opening of the slipper. You need to go all the way around the opening.

Step 16: Continue doing single crochet until you reach the desired height of the ankle. For a warm, snugly bootie you should stop slightly above the ankle.

Step 17: Try the bootie on and see if you like how it fits. If you want the bootie to go higher, you can continue doing more crochet. Otherwise, get ready to fasten the end.

Step 18: As you finish the last row, secure the end by pulling the yarn all the way through the last two loops. And your bootie slipper is done. Do the second pair and don't hesitate to doll your crochet slippers up by adding accessories such as flower, bow or buttons for a fashionable look.

Final Words

These we very basic crochet patterns that are really easy to do by yourself. Crochet slippers are great for the winter season and all of these designs and patterns are also apt for the male version of crochet slippers (minus the embellishments, please). These are also perfect to be gifted to close family members, so have fun making these for yourself and your close ones.

Thank You Page

I want to personally thank you for reading my book. I hope you found information in this book useful and I would be very grateful if you could leave your honest review about this book. I certainly want to thank you in advance for doing this.

If you have the time, you can check my other books too.

Lightning Source UK Ltd.
Milton Keynes UK
UKOW06f1114220415

250102UK00017B/525/P